**READER'S DELIGHT**

# Biography of
# Dhirubhai Ambani

**READER'S DELIGHT**

*An Imprint of Ramesh Publishing House*

**NEW DELHI**

**ISBN  978-93-5012-253-2**

**Published by:** Alok Kumar Gupta *for* Reader's Delight
*(An Imprint of Ramesh Publishing House)*

**Admin. Office:** 12-H, New Daryaganj Road, Opp. Officer's Mess,
New Delhi-110002 ☎ 23261567, 23275224, 23275124

**Showroom:** ● 4457, Nai Sarak, Delhi-6 ☎ 23918938
● Balaji Market, Nai Sarak, Delhi-6 ☎ 23253720, 23282525

**E-Mail:** info@rameshpublishinghouse.com
**Website:** www.rameshpublishinghouse.com

# PREFACE

The biography of Dhirubhai Ambani is truly India's rags to riches story.  He was born in the family of a poor school teacher in a small village and rose to became the one of the biggest business tycoons of India and the world. He built up the only Indian business to feature in the Forbes 500. He is called as the most flamboyant and dynamic business entrepreneurs of India.

He was a man of great vision. He showed a great temperament for business and made exponential growth exploiting every single opportunity. His phenomenal rise in the Indian industry has been one of the most-remarkable events in the Indian Business' history.

He is being widely known and appreciated for shaping the India's equity culture. His pioneering initiative has attracted millions of retail investors in the market which was earlier dominated by select financial institutions. His initiatives and efforts generated billions of rupees for common people who trusted him and his vision.

He was awarded the Indian Entrepreneur of the 20th Century and was regarded as the greatest creator of wealth.

The students of management schools many like to draw lessons from the life of this matriculate with great vision and business acumen.

The inside pages contain an interesting and elevating story of how a poor village boy rose to become the legendary figure in the history of business what the well-established corporate houses of India with abundant resources could not achieve over a period of a century.

**—Publisher**

# CONTENTS


| | |
|---|---|
| Introduction | ... 5 |
| Family History | ... 7 |
| Education | ... 8 |
| Life in Aden | ... 10 |
| Taking Opportunity | ... 14 |
| Marriage | ... 16 |
| Back to India with a Dream | ... 17 |
| His First Enterprise in India | ... 20 |
| The Ambani Magic | ... 23 |
| Reliance – A Dream Come True | ... 25 |
| Rags to Riches | ... 32 |
| First Public offering | ... 33 |
| Master of Bulls & Bears | ... 34 |
| Business Rivalry | ... 36 |
| The Friend & Foe Express | ... 38 |
| The Fatal Stroke | ... 41 |
| Ambani—A Different Mettle | ... 42 |
| Controversies | ... 44 |
| Crusader of Equity Cult | ... 45 |
| The Common Touch—Uncommon vision | ... 46 |
| The Ambani Philosophy | ... 47 |
| The Ambani Connections | ... 48 |
| The Cross-Connection | ... 49 |
| Reliance Sans Dhirubhai | ... 51 |
| Awards and Recognitions | ... 53 |
| Chronology of Events | ... 54 |
| Some Rare Photographs | ... 55 |

# INTRODUCTION

**Dhirubhai Ambani** alias Dhirajlal Hirachand Ambani was the most enterprising Indian entrepreneur. His life journey is reminiscent of the rags to riches story. He is remembered as the one who rewrote Indian corporate history and built a truly global corporate group.

Dhirubhai Ambani built India's largest private sector company and created an equity cult in the Indian capital market. His company, Reliance is the first Indian company to feature in Forbes 500 list.

Dhirubhai Ambani was born on December 28, 1932, at Chorwad, Gujarat. His father was a school teacher. Dhirubhai Ambani started his entrepreneurial career by selling potato fries to pilgrims in Mount Girnar over the weekends.

After doing his matriculation at the age of 16, Dhirubhai moved to Aden, Yemen. He worked there as a gas-station attendant, and as a clerk in an oil company. He returned to India in 1958 with ₹ 50,000 and set up a small trading company.

Dhirubhai Ambani built India's largest private sector company, Reliance India Limited, from a scratch. Over time his business has diversified into a core specialisation in petrochemicals with additional interests in telecommunications, information technology, energy, power, retail, textiles, infrastructure services and capital markets etc.

Dhirubhai Ambani is credited with shaping India's equity culture, attracting millions of retail investors in a market till then dominated by financial institutions. Dhirubhai revolutionised capital markets. From nothing, he generated billions of rupees in wealth for those who put their trust in his companies. With innovative instruments like the convertible debentures, Reliance quickly became a favourite of the stock market in the 1980s.

In 1992, Reliance became the first Indian company to raise money in global markets, its high credit-taking in international markets limited only by India's sovereign rating.

Dhirubhai Ambani was named the Indian Entrepreneur of the 20th Century by the Federation of Indian Chambers of Commerce and Industry (FICCI). A poll conducted by The Times of India in 2000 voted him "greatest creator of wealth in the century".

Dhirubhai Ambani died on July 6, 2002, at Mumbai.

— ✱✱✱ —

# FAMILY HISTORY

His father, Hirachand Ambani was a village school teacher with limited income. He was married twice, having a son from his first marriage (named Samadasbhai) before being widowed. His second

*Dhirubhai with his family*

marriage gave him five more children. Hirachand and Jamnaben had two daughters — Trilochanaben and Jasuben and three sons — Ramnikbhai, Dhirubhai and Natubhai. Dhirubhai was the second son.

The village schoolmaster was a private tutor for several years—a good teacher and 'very strict'. Hirachand Ambani made little money, and lived in extremely austere circumstances in his small village house at Chorwad, Gujarat. He was a Modh Bania by Caste.

— ∗∗∗ —

# EDUCATION

Dhirubhai started his education at the village primary school where his father was a teacher.

In 1945, he moved up to Junagadh and enrolled at the Bahadur Kanji High School. Because of his family's poverty, Dhirubhai was admitted as a free student. He found accommodation in a boarding house funded by the Modh Banias for children of their caste. Dhirubhai did his matriculation in 1949.

Just after Dhirubhai was through his annual matriculation examination and even before the result was out, Hirachandbhai called him home to Chorwad. Hirachandbhai had been unwell for quite some time and had grown extremely weak and frail.

Hirachandbhai told his son the very night he reached home that he had been unwell for past several months, he could not work any more. He knew that Dhirubhai wanted to study further but he could not afford that any more. He needed him to earn for the family. The family needed him to work and earn money. His elder brother, Ramnikbhai had arranged a job for him in Aden, he should go there.

Dhirubhai had really wanted to study for a bachelor's degree, but his ambition melted when he looked into the anxious eyes of his sick father. The very next morning he left for Rajkot to get his passport. Those days Indians did not need a visa for entering Aden but there were rumours around that the no-visa regime was about to change any day. So, he needed to hurry up before the visa rules changed. In a few days he was in Bombay to board the ship to Aden. It was on board the ship that Dhirubhai learnt from a Gujarati newspaper that he had passed his matriculation examination in second division.

With his family still extremely poor, Dhirubhai had no other option but to give up his desire to study more and he reached Aden where his brother Ramnikbhai was working.

# LIFE IN ADEN

Dhirubhai knew the value of time and money, he joined office on the very day of his arrival at Aden. It was a clerk's job with the A. Besse & Co., named after its French founder Antonin Besse. Those days Aden was the second busiest trading and oil bunkering port in the world, after London, handling over 6,300 ships and 1,500 dhows (the traditional wooden sailing vessels of Arabian waters), a year.

A. Besse & Co. was the largest transcontinental trading firm east of Suez in Aden. It was engaged in almost every branch of trading business—cargo booking, handling, shipping, forwarding, and wholesale merchandising. Besse acted as trading agents for a large number of European, American, African and Asian companies and dealt with all sorts of goods ranging from sugar, spices, foodgrains and textiles to office stationary, tools, machinery and petroleum products. Dhirubhai was first sent to the commodities trading section of the firm. Later, he was transferred to the section that handled petroleum products for the oil giant Shell.

While his brother Ramnikbhai kept working in the automotive division, Dhirubhai was transferred to the Shell products division of Besse. As a newly arrived youngster he created an early splash. As he developed more familiarity with the trade, Dhirubhai was sent to market Shell and Burmah lubricants around the Besse network. Some places were not accessible to steamers, so the Besse salesmen would travel by dhow. Lodgings would be extremely rough, and the food difficult for the vegetarian Gujaratis. Dhirubhai was outgoing, robust, and helpful to newcomers. He was physically strong with good physique.

Ramnik was more or less a saintly man. Dhirubhai was a daring one. Dhirubhai's career with Besse was progressing steadily, and the Shell Division was one of the most rapidly expanding areas of company business.

Although he was doing well, Dhirubhai was far from happy with his position as an employee. Right from the beginning he was determined to do something big. He was never comfortable in service. He was a born businessman. He learnt the ways of commodity trading, high seas purchase and sales, marketing and distribution, currency trading, and money management. During lunch break he roamed the souks and bazaars of Aden where traders from numerous different continents and countries bought and sold goods worth millions of pound sterling, the then global currency. Aden was the biggest trading port of the times, a trading port where goods landed from all parts of the world and were dispatched to the farthest corners of different continents. Speculation in manufactured goods and commodities was rife all over the Aden bazaars.

Dhirubhai felt tempted to speculate but had no money for that and was still raw for such trading. To learn the tricks of the trade he offered to work free for a Gujarati trading firm. There he learnt accounting, book keeping, preparing shipping papers and documents, and dealing with banks and insurance companies. Doing business on one's own account was strictly forbidden to Besse employees by the terms of their contract, and his elder brother Ramnikbhai also disapproved that, so Dhirubhai would simply tell he was 'studying the market'.

When he thought he had learnt the basics of commodities trading, Dhirubhai began speculating in high seas purchase and sales of all sorts of goods. He did not have enough money of his own for such speculative trading. So he borrowed as much as he could from friends and small Aden shopkeepers on terms nobody had ever offered them. "Profit we share and all loss will be mine!" became his motto. During lunch break and after office hours he was always in the local bazaar, trading in one thing or the other.

Soon, those around him found that he had an uncanny knack for such speculative trading. He seldom lost money in any deal. He once told a friend, "I think I had an animal instinct about such trading but there was a lot of reading and understanding of market trends behind that animal instinct of mine. I read every bit of paper I could lay my hands on about what was happening around the world, I listened carefully to every word uttered in the market, picked every bit of gossip in the shipping circles and pondered long through the night in the bed about the pros and cons of every deal I wanted to make."

Dhirubhai made some profits, and learned the fundamentals of business and money. But he also made some near disastrous mistakes, which almost wiped out his capital. On one occasion he suffered a tight financial squeeze when an incoming cargo of sugar was damaged by sea-water and his customer refused to accept delivery pending-settlement of his insurance claim, Dhirubhai had to pass the hat among Besse colleagues for loans to bail himself out.

Meantime, the Shell oil refinery and the first oil harbour came up in Aden in 1954, the year Dhirubhai returned home to Gujarat to marry Kokilaben. As expected, A. Besse & Co. became the agents for distribution of Shell refinery products. Dhirubhai had done well at the office during his first five years. Now he was sent on promotion to the oil filling station at the newly built harbour.

He liked the new job, though it was a lot more demanding than his desk job earlier. Here he had to service the ships bunkering for diesel and lubricants. He enjoyed visiting the ships, making friends with sailors and the engine staff. He heard from them first hand accounts of their voyages in different parts of the world of which he had until then read about only in books and magazines. And, here it was that he first began dreaming of one day building a refinery of his own!

— *** —

# TAKING OPPORTUNITIES

At the age of 16, Dhirubhai was physically strong, and already possessed of the persuasiveness that was to mark his later business career. It is tempting to look into the culture of the Modh Bania for an explanation of what his critics see as his ruthless business ethics and 'shamelessness'. But many other entrepreneurs have also sprung from the same background in Kathiawar—most would shrink from the manipulation of the government that became part and parcel of the Ambani operation, even at the cost of less success. The answer lies probably in the deep poverty that his family endured as the cost of his father's devotion to a teaching career. While he also learned that life is a web of relationships and obligations, Dhirubhai was fired with an ambition never to become dependent on anyone or to stay long in somebody else's service.

In the 1950s, the Yemini administration realized that their main unit of currency, the Rial, was disappearing fast. Upon launching an investigation, they realized that a lot of Rials were being routed to the Port City of Aden. It was found that a Gujarati young man in his twenties was placing unlimited buy orders for Yemini Rials.

During those days, the Yemini Rial was made of pure silver coins and was in much demand at the London Bullion Exchange. Young Dhirubhai bought the Rials, melted them into pure silver and sold it to the bullion traders in London.

During the latter part of his life, while talking to reporters, he once said "The margins were small but it was money for jam. After three months, it was stopped. But I made a few lakhs. In short, I was a manipulator. A very good manipulator. But I don't believe in not taking opportunities."

# MARRIAGE

In March 1954, Dhirubhai married at the age of 22, in a match arranged by his mother (his father had died in 1951) but which Dhirubhai himself had supervised. His life partner was Kokilaben Patel, the daughter of a postmaster in Jamnagar, the port on the western side of Kathiawar. Her family was not particularly wealthy. Kokilaben was also a Modh Bania,

*Dhirubhai and Kokilaben*

as the strict caste endogamy of the time demanded and her character complemented that of Dhirubhai, a solid home anchor very much grounded in traditional values and religious piety.

Soon after marriage Dhirubhai returned to Aden to resume his duty there. He now had another reason to work more and earn money to fulfil the needs of additional responsibility and expectations of his wife.

— ✳✳✳ —

# BACK TO INDIA
# WITH A DREAM

By the year 1957, it became clear that the British rule in Aden would not last long in the face of growing Yemeni movement for independence supported by Gamal Abdel Nasser's revolutionary government from across the Suez. The large Indian community of Hindu and Parsi Gujaratis began preparing to move out of Aden. Some began returning home to India, while some chose to settle in Britain. Aden Indians those days were allowed to settle in Britain.

Where to go on leaving Aden was debated among the colony's settlers heatedly everyday. Some of Dhirubhai's friends told him that he should migrate to London where, considering his talents, acumen and guts, he could find better opportunities of growth. At the port and on ships at Aden he often heard glowing accounts of post-war Britain and the promises of a life of much greater ease there than one could ever hope to find in India.

Dhirubhai weighed his options. By now he had saved some money and was thinking of setting up some business of his own. Although Dhirubhai's father had died in 1951, he had in the meantime been blessed with his first son, Mukesh, in April, 1957. Kokilaben and Mukesh were back home in India.The choice of opening a shop somewhere in London was tempting but he felt India was calling him home.

Those were exciting years in India. The country was in the midst of implementing the second five-year Plan which promised to build big industries, raise new big dams across many rivers, lay new roads through the length and breadth of the country, boost agricultural production to new record levels and set up a huge network of foodgrains procurement centers.

Though by the end of 1958, the newspapers coming from India were painting a rather gloomy picture of the country's finances and foreign exchange reserves, there was also a new vigour and a new fervor in their reports of a new ₹ 10,000-crore five-year Plan then under preparation. The Plan promised to open massive new opportunities for growth for the country's youth. Prime Minister Jawaharlal Nehru was daily exhorting the young to cast away their old ways and help build a new India. His words were stirring and roused the passions of every young Indian, especially of those living far away from the country.

Dhirubhai was then 26 years, full of youthful vigour and vitality, and filled with high hopes for himself and for the new India of Nehru's dreams. He just could not miss the excitement of being in India in such tumultuous times.

He decided to return home, instead of going to London to live a life of ease there.

He left Aden in 1958, with his seven years service and right of residency as a failback, to try his hand in business back in India.

At the end of 1958, Dhirubhai returned to India. From all his years with Besse & Co and all his evenings 'studying the market' he had accumulated savings of just 29000 East African shillings—then worth about US$3000 or ₹ 50,000.

# HIS FIRST ENTERPRISE IN INDIA

Dhirubhai Ambani returned to India and started trading business in partnership with Champaklal Damani, his second cousin, who also used to be with him in Aden. The first office of the Reliance Commercial Corporation was set up at the Narsinathan Street in Masjid Bunder. It was 350 sq ft. room with a telephone, one table and three chairs. Initially, they had two assistants to help them with their business. During this period, Dhirubhai and his family used to stay in a one bedroom apartment at the Jaihind Estate in Bhuleshwar, Mumbai.

At the tiny Masjid Bunder office, Dhirubhai began to assemble a team that stayed with him for decades as Reliance grew. They included Meswani, elder brother Ramnikbhai who had also returned from Aden, younger brother Natwarlal (Natubhai) on completing his education. Dhirubhai also enlisted the services of old acquaintances from Aden. Dhirubhai quickly became a familiar figure around the streets of Pydhonie, the synthetic yarn trading district of Bombay.

If cotton and silk had been the materials of India's textile industry right from the old handloom days to the industrial looms of the early 20th century, by the 1950s the industry and its consumers were hungry for the artificial threads created by modern chemical science. Nylon, viscose and polyester were cheap, hardwearing, quick-drying and crease-proof, and could imitate both cotton and silk. The problem for yarn dealers at Pydhonie was not usually to find buyers but to secure supplies. The tightening of industrial controls and import quotas since Independence had choked supply of these 'luxuries'.

India had one viscose factory owned by the Birlas, and one government-owned nylon plant. The first polyester fibre plant did not open until the 1970s. These domestic factories supplied only a small fraction of local demand from textile weavers. Smugglers supplied some of the demand, bringing in yarn by either misdeciaring cargoes at regular ports or simply running small ships to the numerous creeks and beaches of India's west coast. Made-up textiles were also smuggled as well, via Dubai or Singapore. Indian visitors to Japan's artificial textile industries, then in their great postwar expansion phase, recall seeing vast production of sari-length material, for which officially there was no open market in the subcontinent at all. The other source came from the strictly controlled import licences given to registered exporters of textiles, allowing import of raw materials worth a certain percentage of their export earnings. Like many others, Dhirubhai realised that these import or 'replenishment' licences (known as REPS) were as good as money, even though some of them were officially not transferrable and imports had to be made by the 'actual user' of the materials. By paying higher margins than any other traders, Dhirubhai soon became the main player in the market for REP licences.

Dhirubhai's fast pace caused a rift with his partner Champaklal Damani in 1965. Champaklal Damani and Dhirubhai Ambani ended their partnership and Dhirubhai started on his own. It is believed that both had different temperaments and a different take on how to conduct business. While Damani was a cautious trader and did not believe in building yarn inventories, Dhirubhai was a known risk taker and he believed in building inventories, anticipating a price rise, and making profits.

The final rupture came after one clash when, at Dhirubhai's urging, Reliance built up a large holding of yarn in the expectation of a price rise. Damani pressured Dhirubhai to cut back their exposure. So Dhirubhai sold the yarn stockpile-to himself, in secret. Two or three weeks later the price of yarn shot up and Dhirubhai made a killing. Many others among Dhirubhai's trade associates also believe the partners were incompatible.

It is also believed that someone advised Dhirubhai's partner that he had made sufficient money and now should come out as Dhirubhai's business is catching live serpents. Champaklal Damani himself agreed to separate willingly. Damani went into trading in a new company, while Dhirubhai and his brothers paid some ₹ 600,000 to buy him out of Reliance. Soon after, Dhirubhai moved the office to bigger premises in the more central Court House building at Dhobi Talao, Bombay.

— *** —

# THE AMBANI MAGIC

At the Bombay yarn market margins were tiny in the trade itself — but Dhirubhai's dominance also put him in the position of being able to turn on and off much of the supply of yarn into the Indian market. Dhirubhai's intervention in a market crisis in the mid-1960s when spiralling textile prices led government authorities to crack down on 'speculation' in the yarn market by banning forward trading, and then arresting traders found to be continuing the practice. Some people, about a dozen, were arrested in the market. The trading community was despondent as their colleagues languished all day in the cells of the Picket Road Police Station. Approaches to officials by the Bombay Yarn Markets and Exchange Association got nowhere. Then, late in the evening, Dhirubhai arrived like a storm at the police station, shouting greetings to the senior officers, and handing out snacks to everyone. Within an hour, all the arrested traders had been released, and the complaints against them shelved.

Dhirubhai also emerged as saviour of the market when an even greater supply crisis occurred in 1967. On a report that 'actual user' import licences had been traded and misused, the Customs authorities in Bombay under the then Assistant Collector, impounded all incoming cargoes of artificial fibres.

The government insisted that whoever imported the yarn had to be the manufacturer who wove it into cloth. About 40 million rupees (then about US$5.3 million) worth of yarn was seized. Many traders then defaulted on loans taken out to cover the imports. The entire artificial textile market was paralysed. This is when Dhirubhai saved all continuously fighting for about six months. He used to go to lawyers day in and day out. He even went to Delhi to see Morarji Desai (then finance minister). That was the time one could see he was a wizard. He used all the ways and means. The crisis ended as quickly as it started, ostensibly after a one-day hearing of the importers appeal in the Customs, Excise and Gold Appellate Tribunal. That was believed to be the Ambani's magic!

# RELIANCE — A DREAM COME TRUE

After trading in a range of products, primarily spices and fabrics, for eight years, Dhirubhai achieved the first of the many goals he had set for himself when he became the owner of a small spinning mill at Naroda, near Ahmedabad. He did not look back since then.

Within a year of splitting with Champaklal Damani, Dhirubhai took Reliance into textile manufacturing for the first time. He decided to locate it in Gujarat rather than Bombay, because of the cheaper land prices. He settled

*Dhirubhai, Mukesh and Anil at the Reliance Textiles plant inauguration in Naroda, Gujarat, 1977-78.*

on a 10000 square metre plot, in a new industrial estate developed by the Gujarat state government at Naroda, on the fringes of Ahmedabad. By a further stroke of luck the farmers owning some 100 000 square metres of adjacent land were willing to sell. Dhirubhai had a simple factory built, installed four knitting machines, and appointed his brother as plant manager. Dhirubhai was again lucky in that, around this time, the British hold on Aden was becoming more tenuous.

Even ahead of the British withdrawal in 1967, foreign nationals felt threatened by the insurgency mounted by the People's Liberation Front. Many of the Indians working for A Besse & Co decided it was time to go home. So Dhirubhai had a ready-made source of educated managers, accountants and salesmen, drilled to European standards.

The word went around that Dhirubhai would find jobs for his old colleagues, and a dozen old hands from A Besse & Co accepted his offer. Most stayed for the rest of their working careers. None of them knew very much about textile production, however, and it was a case of learning by trial and error. It was very small, only about 20 people in the whole factory, about five or six from Aden. Nobody was familiar with textiles. The first two years, 1966-67, was a very hard time. The product had to be established. They worked from morning to late evening. Dhirubhai was very encouraging, and had a family atmosphere. The employer-employee relationship was not there.

At one time, it appeared the mill would have to close down because Reliance could not sell the cloth it was making. After putting in a full shift at the factory in Naroda, from 7 am to 3 pm, they would spend the afternoons and evenings touring markets around Ahmedabad trying to persuade shopkeepers to stock Reliance fabrics. Dhirubhai worked everyone hard, often calling his managers in Naroda at 6 am from Bombay before they started out to work. They were expected to solve problems on their own initiative. Dhirubhai himself set the example.

At one time, when spare parts were urgently needed for imported machines at Naroda. Dhirubhai had the parts flown in from Germany, and then discovered that no trucks were available for the haul up to Ahmedabad. He immediately bought two trucks, one to carry the parts and one as a backup, and sent up the consignment. The trucks were then sold in Ahmedabad. But he was forgiving of honest mistakes. He used to say, "Nothing to worry-in business, anything can happen."

The result was steady growth in sales and profits for Reliance. In 1967, the first full year of production at Naroda, the company recorded sales of ₹ 9 million in 1967, yielding a net profit of ₹ 1.3 million. Dhirubhai and his family shareholders refused to take dividends and kept ploughing earnings back into more machines. After a decade of manufacturing, in 1977 Reliance had a turnover of ₹ 680 million, and profits of ₹ 105 million.

In 1975, a technical team from the World Bank recognised the Naroda mill as one of the best composite textile mills in India and certified it as 'excellent even by developed country standards'.

In 1977, the company went public. At the time of the Reliance Textiles IPO, participation in the Indian capital markets was largely limited to a small but influential elite which dabbled in a handful of stocks. The great majority of India's middle class chose to stay away. Dhirubhai's decision to prefer the capital markets over banks as the primary source of funding for his ambitious expansion plans, was as daring as it was unprecedented.

In the event, The Reliance IPO was an unlikely success. Against all odds, Dhirubhai managed to convince a sufficiently large number of sceptical middle class investors to put their money, and faith, in what was then a small, relatively unknown company.

In August 1979, the Indian Textile Journal reported on a massive factory at Naroda occupying 230,000 square metres and employing 5000 staff. It had banks of machines for texturising or 'crimping' artificial fibres to give particular sheens, machines for twisting the polyester and nylon fibres into yarns, and machines for weaving the yarns into textiles. The yarns were sold to other Indian textile manufacturers, or used in-house. Most significantly perhaps, Dhirubhai established his own brand name, 'Vimal' (named after a son of his brother Ramnikbhai), by dint of lavish advertising under the slogan 'Only Vimal'. In addition, Dhirubhai had got around the reluctance of established wholesalers and shopkeepers to accept a new brand by creating his own network of shops. Across India, some 400 shops were franchised to sell the Vimal brand of polyester materials for saris, shirts, suits and dresses. Dhirubhai was held in 'high esteem' by his staff, who attributed Vimal's success to his dynamic leadership.

Dame Luck certainly seems to have favoured Dhirubhai. Ever since the emergence of 'Vimal', he had developed the Midas touch. Anything he touched became gold. Anything he started blossomed into success. Dhirubhai Ambani remained in Bombay because manufacturing was only one facet of his business. For a decade, the textile plant at Naroda was supportive and subsidiary to his yarn trading activities. In addition, he was steadily augmenting his skills at breeding money from money, and at wielding political and bureaucratic influence on government policies and their interpretation.

Dhirubhai was never simply an industrialist, a trader, a financial juggler or a political manipulator, but all four in one. From his earliest days in Junagadh, Dhirubhai had learned that relationships were the key to unlocking help, and that the law could be argued with.

The subsequent growth and success of Reliance and its philosophy of generously rewarding shareholders rapidly gave Dhirubhai an iconic status in the Indian financial markets. Under Dhirubhai's charismatic leadership, the Annual General Meetings (AGM) of Reliance took on the character of large public spectacles. Typically held in large public arenas, and attended by thousands of adoring shareholders, the Reliance AGM became a day to remember in the annual corporate calendar of India. In 1986, the Reliance AGM held in Cross Maidan, Mumbai, was attended by as many as 30,000 stockholders—a record in India's corporate history.

By the mid-eighties, Dhirubhai had become something of a living legend, widely hailed by peers and critics alike as one of the greatest corporate visionaries in the history of post-Independent India. But Dhirubhai was never one to rest on his laurels. In the early eighties, he had taken the first important step in strategic backward integration for Reliance with the commissioning of the Patalganga plant which initially manufactured polyester filament yarn and polyester staple fibre. He subsequently diversified into chemicals, petrochemicals, plastics, power. The company as a whole was described by the BBC as "a business empire with an estimated annual turnover of $12bn, and an 85,000-strong workforce". The final phase of Reliance's diversification occurred in the 1990s when the company turned aggressively towards petrochemicals and telecommunications.

In 1991, he set up Reliance Hazira plant, for the manufacture of petrochemicals—the next link in the backward integration chain. At the time, Reliance Hazira plant represented the single largest investment made by a private sector group in India at a single location. Meanwhile, Dhirubhai had firmed up plans of setting up a massive grassroots refinery—the next big leap in his overall strategic roadmap for Reliance. Conceived as the world's largest grassroots refinery at the time, Jamnagar in Gujarat was to have an annual capacity of 27 million tonnes.

In the face of formidable challenges, including a massive cyclone that flattened the project site mid-way through construction, Reliance commissioned the Jamnagar facility in 1999. It was a fully integrated refinery, complete with a dedicated port and a captive supply of power. The refinery was not only commissioned ahead of schedule, but also set up at a cost that was significantly lower than the prevailing global benchmark for a project of such magnitude.

It was one of Dhirubhai's great dreams in life to see ordinary Indians enjoy the enormous economic benefits of being able to access affordable yet world class telecommunications infrastructure. He wanted Reliance to spearhead a communications revolution that would dramatically cut down the cost of connectivity, and propel India into the digital age. His ultimate ambition— To make the cost of a phone call cheaper than that of a post card. It was therefore entirely logical for Reliance to enter the telecommunications space when the sector was opened up for private participation in the 1990s.

The rest, as they say, is history. Today, Reliance Communications is India's largest information and communications services provider with over 20 million subscribers, and offers the full range of integrated telecom services—at prices that are, by far, the lowest anywhere in the world.

— *** —

# RAGS TO RICHES

On their move to Bombay, Dhirubhai and his young family had moved into an apartment on the 3rd floor of the Jal Hind Society building in Bhuleshwar, a very crowded district of shops, markets and residential tenements in the central part of the city. The building is what is known as a chawl in Bombay—numerous small apartments, often just single rooms, opening on to open galleries around a central courtyard which is set back from the street behind commercial premises. Quite often the toilets and washing facilities are shared at ground level. The flat, had two small bedrooms, a living room, kitchen and internal bathroom in 1958. Being 'quite luxurious' compared to the single rooms many Gujarati families had to occupy in Bombay at that time. Even so, Dhirubhai and his young family, eventually two boys and two girls, lived austerely in surroundings that were crowded, noisy and dirty.

After ten years at Bhuleshwar, in 1968, Dhirubhai moved his home out of the chawl to a more comfortable flat in Altamount Road, one of the city's elite areas on a hill overlooking the Arabian Sea. Fond of driving fast, Dhirubhai had first bought a Fiat car, and then moved on to a Mercedes-Benz. Later, in the 1970s, he indulged a taste for flashy automobiles by acquiring a Cadillac, one of the very few in the country then and even now.

— *** —

# FIRST PUBLIC OFFERING

Dhirubhai decided that unlike most Indian businessmen who borrowed heavily from financial institutions to nurture their entrepreneurial ambitions, he would instead raise money from the public at large to fund his industrial ventures. In 1977, Reliance Industries went public and raised equity capital from tens of thousands of investors, many of them located in small towns. From then onwards, Dhirubhai started extensively promoting his company's textile brand name, 'Vimal'. The story goes that on one particular day, the Reliance group chairman inaugurated the retail outlets of as many as 100 franchises.

Dhirubhai Ambani is awarded with starting the equity cult in India. More than 58,000 investors from various parts of India subscribed to Reliance's IPO in 1977. Dhirubhai was able to convince large number of small investors from rural Gujarat that being shareholders of his company would be profitable.

Reliance Industries was the first private sector company whose Annual General Meetings were held in stadiums. In 1986, The Annual General Meeting of Reliance Industries number of first-time retail investors to invest in Reliance. Ambani's net worth was estimated at about ₹ 1 billion by early 1980s.

— ******* —

# MASTER OF BULLS AND BEARS

In 1982, Reliance Industries came up with a rights issue regarding partly convertible debentures. It was rumoured that company was making all efforts to ensure that their stock prices did not slide an inch. Sensing an opportunity, a Bear Cartel which was a group of stock brokers from Calcutta started short-selling the shares of Reliance. To counter this, a group of stock brokers believed to be 'Friends of Reliance' started buying the short-sold shares of Reliance Industries on the Bombay Stock Exchange.

The Bear Cartel was acting on the belief that the Bulls would be short of cash to complete the transactions and would be ready for settlement under the *'Badla'* trading system operative in the Bombay Stock Exchange. The bulls kept on buying and a price of ₹ 152 per share was maintained till the day of settlement. On the day of settlement, the Bear Cartel was taken aback when the Bulls demanded a physical delivery of shares. To complete the transaction, the much needed cash was provided to the stock brokers who had bought shares of Reliance, by none other than Dhirubhai Ambani. In the case of non-settlement, the Bulls demanded an *'Unbadla'* (a penalty sum) of ₹ 35 per share. With this, the demand increased and the shares of Reliance shot above ₹ 180 in minutes. The settlement caused an enormous uproar in the market.

To find a solution to this situation, the Bombay Stock Exchange was closed for three business days. Authorities from the Bombay Stock Exchange (BSE) intervened in the matter and brought down the '*Unbadla*' rate to ₹ 2 with a stipulation that the Bear Cartel had to deliver the shares within the next few days. The Bear Cartel bought shares of Reliance from the market at higher price levels and it was also learnt that Dhirubhai Ambani himself supplied those shares to the Bear Cartel and earned a healthy profit out of the Bear Cartel's misadventure.

After this incident, many quesstions were raised by his detractors and the press. Not many people were able to understand as to how a yarn trader till a few years ago was able to get in such a huge amount of cash flow during a crisis period. The answer to this was provided by the then finance minister, Pranab Mukherjee in the parliament. He informed the house that a Non-Resident Indian had invested ₹ 22 Crore in Reliance during 1982-83. These investments were routed through many companies. These companies were primarily registered in Isle of Man. The interesting factor was that all the promoters or owners of these companies had a common surname 'Shah'. An investigation by the Reserve Bank of India in the incident did not find any unethical or illegal acts or transactions committed by Reliance or its promoters.

— ✳✳✳ —

# BUSINESS RIVALRY

Nusli Wadia of Bombay Dyeing was, at one point in time, the biggest competitor of Dhirubhai and Reliance Industries. Both Nusli Wadia and Dhirubhai were known for their influence in the political circles and their ability to get the most difficult licenses approved during the times of pre-liberalized economy. During the Janata Party rule between 1977 - 1979, Nusli Wadia obtained the permission to build a 60,000 tonnes per annum Dimethyl terephthalate (DMT) plant. Before the letter of intent was converted into a licence, many hurdles came in the way. Finally, in 1981, Nusli Wadia was granted the license for the plant. This incident acted as a catalyst between the two parties and the competition took an ugly turn.

The mid-eighties were a period during which the Reliance group got locked in a bitter turf battle with Bombay Dyeing headed by Nusli Wadia. The two corporate groups were producing competing products—Reliance was manufacturing purified terephthalic acid (PTA) and Bombay Dyeing, di-methyl terephthalate (DMT). Wadia lost the battle and reportedly became the source of information for many of the articles against the Ambanis that subsequently appeared in The Indian Express. In

1985, the Mumbai police accused a general manager in a Reliance group company of conspiring to kill Wadia, a charge that was never established in a court of law. Many years later, a newspaper owned by the Ambanis would accuse Wadia of illegally holding two passports and played up the fact that he was Mohammed Ali Jinnah's grandson.

— ✳✳✳ —

# THE FRIEND
# AND FOE EXPRESS

At one point in time, Ramnath Goenka (owner of The Indian Express) was a friend of Dhirubhai Ambani. Ramnath Goenka was also considered to be close to Nusli Wadia. On many occasions, Ramnath Goenka tried to intervene between the two warring factions and bring an end to the enmity. Later on, Ramnath Goenka chose to support Nusli Wadia.

As days passed by, The Indian Express, a national daily published by him, carried a series of articles against Reliance Industries and Dhirubhai in which they claimed that Dhirubhai was using unfair trade practices to maximise the profits. Ramnath Goenka did not use his staff at the Indian Express to investigate the case but assigned his close confidante, advisor and chartered accountant S. Gurumurthy for this task. Apart from S. Gurumurthy, another journalist Maneck Davar, who was not on the rolls of Indian Express, started contributing stories. Jamnadas Moorjani, a businessman opposed to the Ambanis was also a part of this campaign.

Both Ambani and Goenka were equally criticized and admired by sections of the society. People criticized Goenka that he was using a national newspaper for the cause of a personal enmity. Critics believed that there were many other businessman in the country who were using more unfair and unethical practices but Goenka chose to target only Ambani and not the others. Critics also admired Goenka for his ability to run these articles without any help from his regular staff. Dhirubhai Ambani was also getting more recognition and admiration, in the meantime. A section of the public started appreciating Dhirubhai's business sense and his ability to tame the system according to his wishes.

The end to this tussle came only after Dhirubhai Ambani suffered a stroke. While Dhirubhai Ambani was recovering in San Diego, his sons Mukesh and Anil Ambani managed the affairs. The Indian Express had turned the guns against Reliance and was directly blaming the government for not doing enough to penalize Reliance Industries.

The battle between Wadia, Goenka and the Ambanis took a new direction and became a national crisis. Gurumurthy and another journalist, Mulgaokar consorted with President Giani Zail Singh and ghost-wrote a hostile letter to the Prime Minister Rajiv Gandhi on his behalf. The Indian Express published a draft of the President's letter as a scoop, not realizing that Zail Singh had made changes to the letter before sending it to Rajiv Gandhi. Ambani had won the battle at this point. Now, while the tussle was directly between the Prime Minister Rajiv Gandhi and Ramnath Goenka, Ambani made a quiet exit.

The government then raided the Express guest house in New Delhi's Sunder Nagar and found the original draft of the letter with corrections in Mulgaokar's handwriting. By 1988-89, Rajiv's government retaliated with a series of prosecutions against the Indian Express. Even then, Goenka retained his iconic stature because, to many people, he seemed to be replaying his heroic defiance during the Emergency regime of Indira Gandhi.

# THE FATAL STROKE

Dhirubhai Ambani was admitted to the Breach Candy Hospital in Mumbai on June 24, 2002 after he suffered a major 'brain stroke'. This was his second stroke, the first one had occurred in February 1986 and had kept his right hand paralyzed. He was in a state of coma for more than a week. A battery of doctors were unable to save his life. He breathed his last on July 6, 2002, at around 11:50 pm.

*Dhirubhai with sons Mukesh and Anil*

His funeral procession was not only attended by top business people, politicians and celebrities but also by thousands of ordinary people. His elder son, Mukesh Ambani performed the last rites as per Hindu traditions. He was cremated at the Chandanwadi Crematorium in Mumbai at around 4:30 pm on July 7, 2002.

He is survived by Kokilaben Ambani, his wife, two sons, Mukesh Ambani and Anil Ambani, and two daughters, Nina Kothari and Deepti Salgaocar.

At the time of Dhirubhai's death, Reliance Group had a gross turnover of ₹ 75,000 Crore or USD $ 15 Billion.

— *** —

# AMBANI — A DIFFERENT METTLE

Dhirubhai Ambani achieved what almost everybody would consider impossible. In a life spanning 69 years, he built from scratch India's largest privately controlled corporate empire. He would often say that success was his biggest enemy. He was a man who aroused extreme responses in others. Either you loved him or you hated him. There was just no way you could have been indifferent to this amazing entrepreneur who thought big, acted tough, knew how to bend rules or have rules bent for him. He was a visionary as well as a manipulator, a man who communicated with the rich and the poor with equal felicity, who was generous beyond the call of duty with those whom he liked and utterly ruthless with his rivals—a man of many parts, of irreconcilable contrasts and paradoxes galore.

One could not ask for a more spectacular 'rags-to-riches' tale. The first job Dhirubhai held in Aden was that of an attendant in a gas station. Half a century later, he would become chairman of a company that owned the largest oil refinery in India and the fifth largest in the world—Reliance Petroleum Limited at Jamnagar that has an annual capacity to refine up to 27 million tonnes of crude oil.

When he died, the Reliance group of companies that Dhirubhai led had a gross annual turnover in the region of ₹ 75,000 crore or close to US $ 15 billion. The group's interests include the manufacture of synthetic fibres, textiles and petrochemical products, oil and gas exploration,  petroleum refining, besides telecommunications and financial services.

In 1976-77, the Reliance group had an annual turnover of ₹ 70 crore. Fifteen years later, this figure had jumped to ₹ 3,000 crore. In a period of 25 years, the value of the Reliance group's assets had jumped from ₹ 33 crore to ₹ 30,000 crore. By the turn of the century, this amount had skyrocketed to ₹ 60,000 crore.

— *** —

# CONTROVERSIES

Dhirubhai Ambani's meteoric rise was not without its fair share of controversy. In India and in most countries of the world, there exists a close nexus between business and politics. In the days of the licence control raj Dhirubhai, more than many of his fellow industrialists, understood and appreciated the importance of 'managing the environment', a euphemism for keeping politicians and bureaucrats happy. He made no secret of the fact that he did not have an ego when it came to paying obeisance before government officials—be they of the rank of secretary to the Government of India or a lowly peon.

Long before Dhirubhai entered the scene, Indian politicians were known to curry favour with businessmen —licences and permits would be farmed out in return for handsome donations during election campaigns. The crucial difference in the business-politics nexus lay in the fact that by the time the Reliance group's fortunes were on the rise, the Indian economy had become much more competitive. Hence, it was insufficient for those in power to merely promote the interests of a particular business group; competitors had to simultaneously be put down. This was precisely what happened to the rivals of the Ambanis.

— *** —

# CRUSADER OF EQUITY CULT

While Dhirubhai did not have too many scruples when it came to currying favour with politicians and bureaucrats, what cannot be denied is the fact that perhaps no businessman in India attracted the kind of adulation he did. He successfully convinced close to four million citizens, most of them belonging to the middle class, to invest their hard-earned savings in Reliance group companies. He was fond of describing Reliance shareholders as 'family members' and the group's annual general meetings acquired the atmosphere of large melas attended by hordes.

What cannot also be refuted is the fact that the Reliance group believed in rewarding its shareholders handsomely. Much of the credit for the spread of the so-called 'equity cult' in India in recent years should rightfully go to Dhirubhai, even if the Reliance group was often accused of manipulating share prices. Two group companies Reliance Poly-Ethylene and Reliance Poly-Propylene—went to the extent of blandly stating in the fine print of their public issue prospectus documents that the value of the shares of the companies had been increased through thin and circular trading.

— ∗∗∗ —

# THE COMMON TOUCH — UNCOMMON VISION

Dhirubhai's supporters like to recall instances of his 'common touch' and his ability to interact with individuals from different walks of life. In 1983, he had hosted a lunch for 12,000 of his company's workers on the occasion of the marriage of his younger daughter Dipti.

He would often wonder aloud that if he could achieve what he did in a lifetime, why could a thousand Dhirubhais not flourish. He was sure that there were at least one thousand individuals like him in the country who would dare to dream big. And if all these entrepreneurs could achieve their ambitions, India would become an economic superpower one day, he would aspire.

Dhirubhai's managerial skills were undoubtedly exceptional and he would repose his faith in professionals, many of whom had earlier worked in much-maligned public sector organisations. Whether it was the building of the petroleum refinery at Jamnagar in three years at a capital cost that was 30 per cent lower than comparable projects, or the restarting of the Patalganga plant in one month's time after cyclone and sudden floods had occurred in July 1989, the Reliance management team displayed their competence on many occasions.

— ✳✳✳ —

# THE AMBANI PHILOSOPHY

Dhirubhai's philosophy was to cultivate everybody from the doorkeeper up. In the India of economic plans and government control of the commanding heights that had developed by the 1960s, a lot of grovelling was required for businessmen to get the clearances they needed. Inevitably, the bureaucratic signature needed to move a file from desk to desk came to have a price on it as well. After getting on his feet back in Bombay, Dhirubhai used to make frequent trips to New Delhi. He frequently went in the company of Murli Deora, a fellow yarn trader who was then working his way up in the Congress Party in Bombay. Dhirubhai and Deora used to catch an early flight up to Delhi, and park their bags with a helpful clerk at the Ashoka Hotel while they did their rounds of politicians and bureaucrats to speed up decisions on import licences. Too poor to afford an overnight stay, they would collect their bags and fly back to Bombay the same evening. Later, Dhirubhai could afford to keep a room ready at the Ashoka. His nephew Rasik Meswani also came into the lobbying activity, and eventually selected a canny South Indian, V. Balusubramaniam, as full-time lobbyist for Reliance in New Delhi. Gradually Dhirubhai also learned the channels for large-scale political donations in the top echelons.

— *** —

# THE AMBANI CONNECTIONS

Over the years, Dhirubhai developed close ties with politicians in many parties. The links were not always based on money, however. Dhirubhai is widely acknowledged to be a masterful exponent of his own business visions, which have generally been more far-sighted than those of almost anyone else among India's business leaders. He was quick to grasp that many Indian politicians, officials and bankers could be captivated by intellectual excitement or flattery at being in the inner circle of such an emerging tycoon. Should such individuals later show signs of self-interest or personal financial difficulty, Dhirubhai or one of his lieutenants would pick up the signals. A post-retirement job, a business opportunity for a child, indirect funding or a burst of inspired publicity might then follow for the person concerned.

Dhirubhai also played on the perception that he was an outsider and 'upstart' who deserved help to break through the glass ceilings of vested interest and privilege in the business community. There was an inner circle in the 'Licence Raj'—the allocation by New Delhi of licences to set up factories and expand production capacity.

— ✳✳✳ —

# THE CROSS-CONNECTION

Vishwanath Pratap Singh was one of the few politicians who took on the Ambanis. In May 1985, as finance minister in Rajiv Gandhi's government, he suddenly shifted imports of PTA from the OGL (Open General Licence) category. At that juncture, Reliance needed to import this product to manufacture polyester filament yarn. It was found that the group had 'persuaded' a number of banks to open letters of credit that would allow it to import almost one full year's requirement of PTA on the eve of the issuance of the government notification changing the category under which PTA could be imported. It was hardly a coincidence that soon after V. P. Singh fell out with Rajiv Gandhi, various tax agencies of the Indian government raided the premises of the Express group, a detractor of Ambani.

Things got difficult for the Ambanis after V.P. Singh became prime minister in December 1989. In 1990, government-owned financial institutions like the Life Insurance Corporation and the General Insurance Corporation stonewalled attempts by the Reliance group to acquire managerial control over Larsen and Toubro, one of India's largest construction and engineering companies. Sensing defeat, the Ambanis resigned from the board of the company after incurring huge losses. Dhirubhai, who had become L&T chairman in April 1989, had to quit his post to make way for D. N. Ghosh, former chairman of the State Bank of India.

Once again, in an ironical twist of fate, more than eleven years later, the Reliance group suddenly sold its stake in L&T to Grasim Industries headed by Kumaramangalam Birla. This transaction too attracted adverse attention. Questions were raised about how the Reliance group had increased its stake in L&T a short while before the sale to Grasim had taken place. The watchdog of the stock markets, the Securities and Exchange Board of India (SEBI) instituted an inquiry into the transactions following allegations of price manipulation and insider trading. Reliance had to later cough up a token fine imposed by SEBI.

These are hardly the only controversies involving the Reliance group. Two senior executives of the Reliance group, including one who was known to be close to Dhirubhai, have been accused of violating the Official Secrets Act after a Cabinet note was found in their office during a police raid. One of these executives reportedly had links with a mafia don. Earlier, there had been a major uproar in the stock exchanges over alleged cases of 'switching' of shares and the issue of duplicate shares. Some of these transactions pertained to Dhirubhai's personal physiotherapist.

— ✳✳✳ —

# RELIANCE SANS DHIRUBHAI

After the death of Dhirubhai Ambani differences cropped up between the two brothers—Mukesh and Anil Ambani over the ownership issue of the Reliance business empire.

In November, 2004, Mukesh Ambani in an interview, admitted to having differences with his brother Anil over 'ownership issues.' He also said that the differences are in the private domain. He was of the opinion that this will not have any bearing on the functioning of the company saying Reliance is one of the strongest professionally-managed companies. Considering the importance of Reliance Industries to the Indian economy, this issue and got an extensive coverage in the media.

K.V. Kamath, the then Managing Director of ICICI Bank was seen in media, a close friend of the Ambani family who helped to settle the issue. The brothers had entrusted their mother, Kokilaben Ambani, to resolve the issue. On June 18, 2005, Kokilaben Ambani announced the settlement through a press release.

The Reliance empire was split between the Ambani brothers, Mukesh Ambani getting RIL and IPCL and his younger sibling Anil Ambani heading Reliance Capital, Reliance Energy and Reliance Infocom. The entity headed by Mukesh Ambani is referred to as the Reliance Industries Limited whereas Anil's Group has been renamed Reliance Anil Dhirubhai Ambani Group (Reliance ADA Group).

Reliance Institute of Life Sciences, a Dhirubhai Ambani Foundation Initiative, was established to promote higher education in various fields of life sciences and related technologies.

After the Reliance group split between the two brothers there was a period of non-communication and conflict of business interests among the two brothers. However, after a long gap there are visible signs of a family reunion recently at their native house at Chorwad, Gujarat when all the Ambani family members spent few days together.

# AWARDS AND RECOGNITIONS

- June 1998 – **'Dean's Medal'** by The Wharton School, University of Pennsylvania, for setting an outstanding example of leadership. Dhirubhai Ambani has the rare distinction of being the first Indian to get Wharton School Dean's Medal.
- 2000, 1998 and 1996 – Featured among **'Power 50 - the most powerful people in Asia'** by Asiaweek magazine.
- A poll conducted by The Times of India in 2000 voted Him **'Greatest Creator of Wealth In The Centuries'**.
- November 2000 – Conferred **'Man of the Century'** award by Chemtech Foundation and Chemical Engineering World in recognition of his outstanding contribution to the growth and development of the chemical industry in India.
- August 2001 – The Economic Times Award for Corporate Excellence for **'Lifetime Achievement'**.
- Dhirubhai Ambani was named the **'Man of 20th Century'** by the Federation of Indian Chambers of Commerce and Industry (FICCI).

— ✱✱✱ —

# CHRONOLOGY OF EVENTS

| | |
|---|---|
| ■ Dhirubhai Ambani born at Chorwad, Gujarat | : 28 Dec., 1932 |
| ■ Moved to Junagadh for Studies | : 1945 |
| ■ Done Matriculation | : 1949 |
| ■ Left for Aden for work | : 1949 |
| ■ Father expired | : 1951 |
| ■ Married to Kokilaben Patel | : March 1954 |
| ■ Son, Mukesh Ambani born | : April, 1957 |
| ■ Left Aden job & returned Bombay | : 1958 |
| ■ Started trading business in Bombay | : 1958 |
| ■ Started yarn-trading business | : 1962 |
| ■ Ended Partnership with C.L. Damani | : 1965 |
| ■ Built Textiles Factory at Naroda | : 1966 |
| ■ World Bank Team visited Reliance Plant | : 1975 |
| ■ First Public Issue of Reliance | : 1977 |
| ■ Only Vimal Campaign | : 1979 |
| ■ Reliance becomes people's favourite at Stock Market | : 1980 |
| ■ Rights Issue of Reliance | : 1982 |
| ■ Business Rivalry with Nusli Wadia | : 1982 |
| ■ The Indian Express campaign against Ambani | : 1982 |
| ■ Problems with V.P. Singh Government | : 1985 |
| ■ Reliance AGM at Bombay attended by 30,000 persons (A record) | : 1986 |
| ■ L&T problem during V.P. Singh's tenure | : 1989 |
| ■ Built Reliance Plant at Hazira | : 1991 |
| ■ Reliance becomes first Indian Company to raise money in global markets | : 1992 |
| ■ Commissioned Jamnagar refinery | : 1999 |
| ■ Dhirubhai Ambani Expired at Mumbai | : 6 July, 2002 |

— *** —

# SOME RARE PHOTOGRAPHS

Dhirubhai Ambani's first office

Dhirubhai Ambani's old house kitchen

Dhirubhai, Kokilaben and sons Mukesh & Anil

Dhirubhai Ambani with Kokilaben

Dhirubhai Ambani's old flat in Mumbai

Dhirubhai Ambani's first car

Dhirubhai Ambani's whole family

Dhirubhai at dinner with Smt. Indira Gandhi

Dhirubhai Ambani and sons Mukesh & Anil

Dhirubhai & sons with U.S. President Bill Clinton

Kokilaben Dhirubhai Ambani Hospital

Reliance Industries Plant